Sharks

FOUR WINDS PRESS   NEW YORK

Sharks

by Ann McGovern

pictures by Murray Tinkelman

For Jim, a superb diver, who introduced me to my first shark

The author acknowledges with thanks the invaluable assistance given by Dr. Eugenie Clark, professor of zoology, University of Maryland.

Library of Congress Cataloging in Publication Data
McGovern, Ann.
 Sharks.
 Includes index.
 SUMMARY: Easy-to-read text and pictures answer basic questions about sharks.
 1. Sharks—Juvenile literature. [1. Sharks]
I. Tinkelman, Murray. II. Title.
QL638.9.M33 597'.31 76–17122
ISBN 0–590–07468–7

Published by Four Winds Press
A Division of Scholastic Magazines, Inc., New York, N.Y.
Text copyright © 1976 by Ann McGovern
Illustrations copyright © 1976 by Murray Tinkelman

CONTENTS

How long have sharks been around?

There were sharks 350 million years ago. Before there were dinosaurs, there were sharks.

Dinosaurs died out about 70 million years ago. But the sharks lived on. Sharks of long long ago looked much like sharks of today.

great white shark

What does a shark look like?

Here is a picture of a shark. A shark is a fish. It lives in water and breathes through gills like all fish.

Most fish have skeletons made of true bones. But sharks are not bony fish. Their skeletons are made of something softer called *cartilage*. (The "bones" in the end of your nose are made of cartilage.)

Most sharks give birth to live baby sharks instead of laying eggs.

A shark's skin looks smooth and slippery. If you stroke a shark one way, it will feel smooth. But if you stroke it the other way, ouch! Your hand may be cut and bleeding.

A shark's body is covered with a hard material that looks—and feels—like bits of sharp teeth.

nurse shark

tiger shark

thresher shark

hammerhead shark

Do all sharks look alike?

No. There are about 250 different kinds of sharks. Here is what some of them look like.

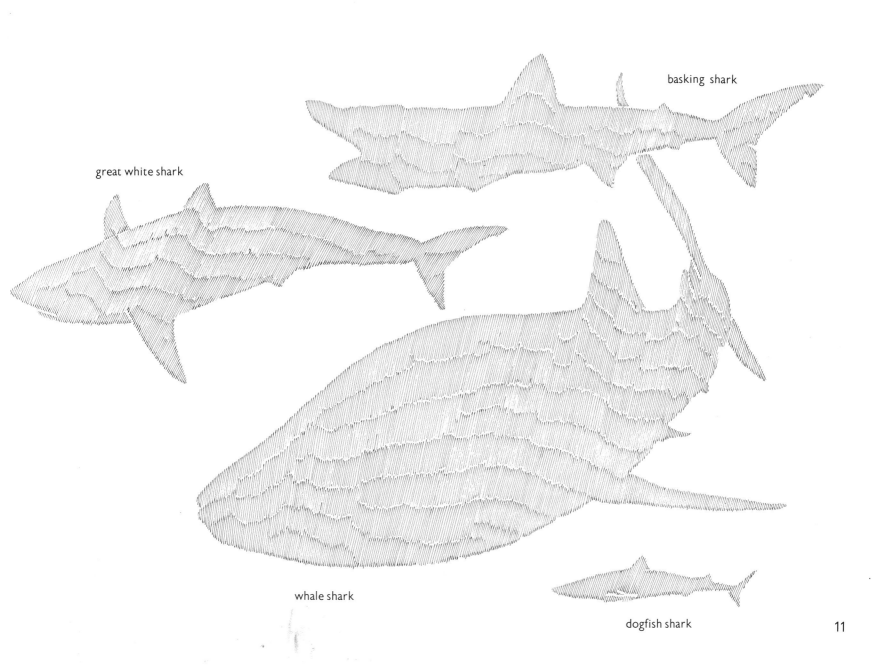

basking shark

great white shark

whale shark

dogfish shark

11

When do sharks attack people?

Shark experts do not know all the answers. But they agree on these four:

A large shark may attack someone if it is very hungry. (You don't have to worry about small sharks.)

Sharks mate at certain times of the year. A person swimming in the water where sharks are mating may be attacked.

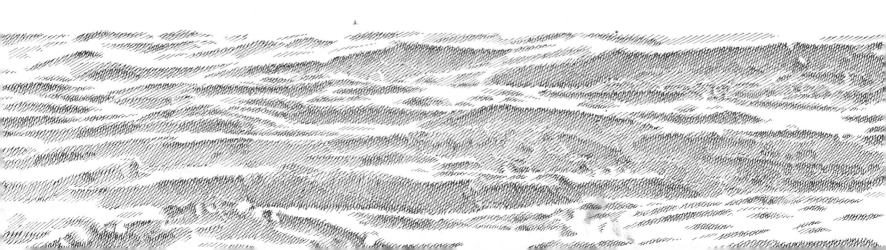

A fish struggling on a fisherman's line sets the water in motion. The water *vibrates*. These *vibrations* bring sharks swimming in from far away. The smell of blood in the water attracts sharks, too. So it's not wise to hold a bleeding, struggling fish in the water. The shark might aim for the fish but bite the person by mistake.

Even harmless sharks will sometimes attack if they are annoyed. Once a diver was showing off to his friends. He caught a nurse shark by the tail, then let it go. Suddenly the nurse shark turned and bit him on the leg.

Are all sharks dangerous?

No.

Most sharks seem to be afraid of people.

Many scuba divers say that the sharks they meet swim away from *them*!

Of course, sharks can be a real danger. But it is a much smaller danger than most people think.

Of all the different kinds of sharks in the world, only about 30 kinds are dangerous.

What sharks are most dangerous?

Some people call the *great white shark* "white death." It is the most dangerous shark but hardly anyone ever sees it. It does not often come into shallow waters where most people swim.

mako shark

The *bull shark* does come into shallow water. It has probably attacked more people than any other shark.

The *mako shark* is one of the fastest sharks in the sea. People don't have time to swim to safety if a mako shark is after them.

Other dangerous sharks are the *blue shark,* the *tiger shark,* and the strange-looking *hammerhead shark.*

The *carpet shark* (sometimes called *wobbegong shark*) is found in Australia. It rests on the bottom of the sea by day. Its colors look so much like part of the sea bottom that sometimes a swimmer steps right on the shark. Then the shark is likely to attack the swimmer.

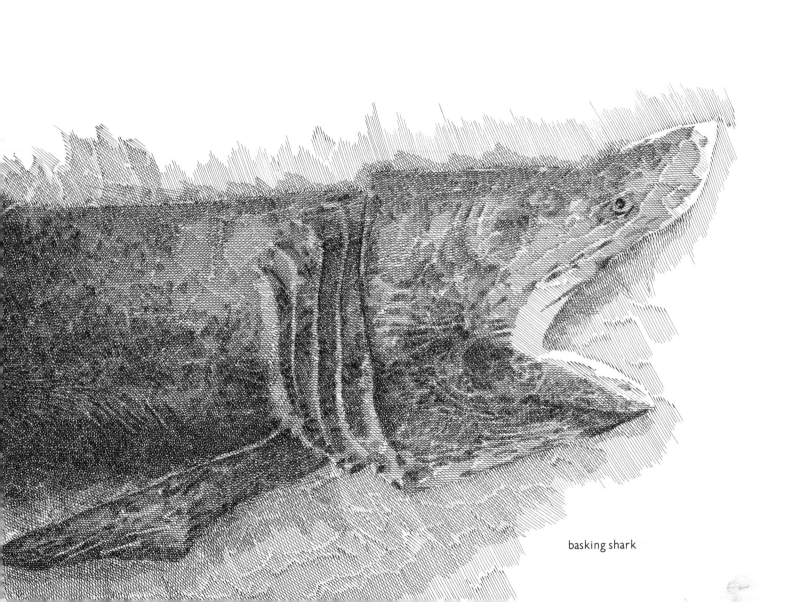

basking shark

What sharks are harmless?

It would take pages and pages to list all the harmless sharks in the world. There would be more than 200 different kinds in the list.

The biggest fish in the world is a *whale shark,* and it is not likely to attack anyone. Swimmers have even taken rides on the back of a whale shark. Whale sharks feed on small fish and on *plankton*—the tiniest living things in the sea.

Another harmless giant is the *basking shark.* It has hardly any teeth!

Sometimes a harmless shark turns mean.

Sometimes one kind of shark is more dangerous in one place than in another. Scientists do not know why.

What is the biggest shark and what is the smallest shark?

The whale shark is the biggest shark. It is also the biggest fish in the world. It grows to 50 feet long—bigger than two big station wagons. It weighs 15 tons! That's how much six big cars weigh.

The smallest adult shark can fit in the palm of your hand. It is only four or five inches long.

The Japanese named it

t s u r a n a g a k o b i t o z a m e .

The word means "the dwarf shark with a long face." The name on this page is as long as the shark!

whale shark

Where do sharks live?

Sharks live in waters all over the world. Almost all sharks live in oceans. A few sharks live in warm rivers and bays. The bull shark sometimes goes back and forth from the ocean to the rivers—mostly in the hotter places of the world.

Most sharks are found in warm waters, but some kinds of sharks live in cold waters and a few kinds even live in icy waters.

Some scientists think that sharks may move to warmer waters at certain times of the year.

What do baby sharks look like?

Shark babies are fully formed when they are born. They look like small copies of adult sharks.

Shark babies are called *pups*.

Some sharks have only one or two pups at a time. Other sharks can have as many as 100.

A tiger shark has about 40 or 50 pups. Each one is about two feet long —about as long as a full-grown cat.

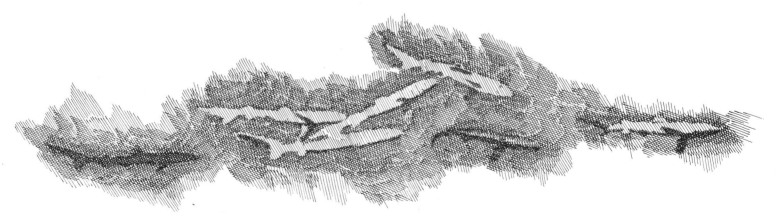

blue shark pups

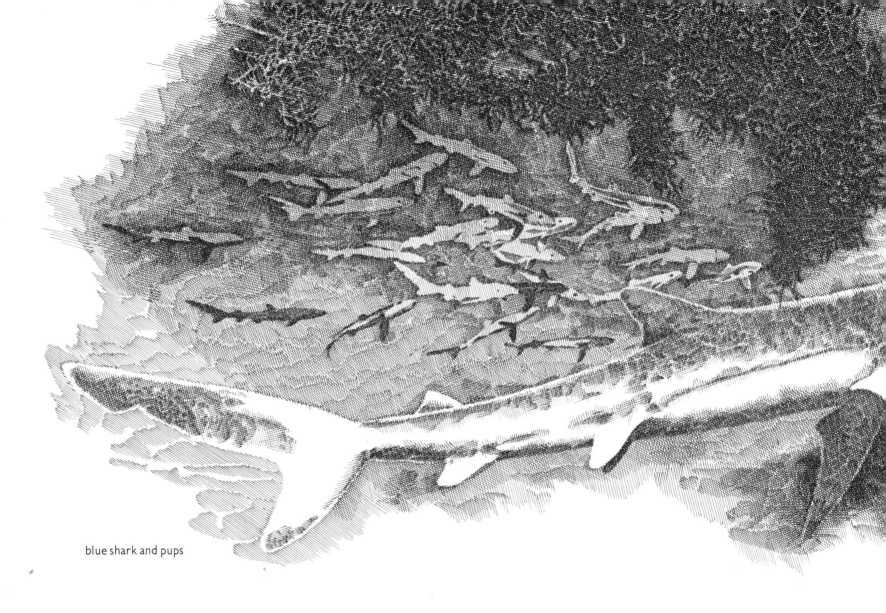

blue shark and pups

How does the mother shark care for her pups?

She doesn't. Shark pups are on their own the minute they are born.

They are born knowing how to swim. They are born with teeth, and they can defend themselves right away!

A mother shark does not eat right after her pups are born. This is probably a good thing for the shark pups. What if she ate some of her babies?

Soon the mother shark leaves her pups and swims away.

Some pups are born in shallow waters. When the mother shark leaves, the pups stay behind to eat and grow. When winter comes, they may travel to warmer waters. No adult shark travels with them.

Do sharks eat other sharks?

Yes. Small sharks are often part of a large shark's meal. And some large sharks, like the hammerhead, eat other large sharks.

When the water is churned up, the vibrations in the water can start a "feeding frenzy." Sharks race in from all directions.

They go wild. They may attack anything they can reach. They have been known to rush at a ship's propeller and to chew up wooden oars of a boat.

If a shark is bitten or slashed by some shark's fin, other sharks will turn on it. They may attack it and eat it even if it is one of their own kind.

What else do sharks eat?

A shark's favorite food is freshly killed fish—or a dolphin if the shark can find a dead or a wounded one.

Healthy dolphins and many big fish are usually too fast for a shark to catch. But when these creatures are wounded or dying—or are too young to defend themselves—they may become a meal for some shark.

dolphin

hammerhead shark

The great white shark can eat creatures half its own size. One 15-foot great white shark was captured with two whole sandbar sharks inside it. Each of them was as big as a grown person.

When there is not enough fresh fish around, sharks may gobble anything.

The tiger shark will swallow almost anything that will fit into its mouth. Inside one tiger shark, fishermen found a leather wallet (without any money), a broken alarm clock, and a collection of nuts and bolts.

Hammerhead sharks will often eat sting rays. The tail of a sting ray has one or two poisonous spines, but that doesn't seem to bother the hammerhead!

sand tiger shark

How often do sharks have to eat?

Most all sharks can go for a long time without food—because of their liver.

A shark's liver is full of oil and fats. These oils and fats can keep a shark going for a long time—sometimes for months.

How do sharks find their food?

A shark uses all of its senses to find its food—smelling, seeing, hearing, touching, and feeling.

A shark's sense of smell is very sharp. It can follow the smell of blood across miles of ocean and find exactly where it's coming from.

Sharks use their eyes to hunt for food, too. Sharks can see 50 feet away in clear water. (Eight motorcycles in a row measure about fifty feet.)

Sharks see better in dim light than in bright light. Maybe that's why they hunt for food mostly at dawn and after sunset.

You can't see a shark's ears because they are inside the shark's head.

Scientists made tests to learn about the shark's sense of hearing. The scientists put a microphone into the water. They taped the sounds made by a big fish that was thrashing around.

Then they played back the tapes through underwater loudspeakers. Sharks rushed in and swam directly to where the sounds were coming from.

tiger shark

Every shark has a kind of combination sense of hearing and sense of feeling. This is due to its *lateral line system,* which runs along the shark's body and onto its head. The lateral line system helps the shark hear and feel vibrations made by a fish moving as far as 100 feet away.

A shark will sometimes bump into a fish before he eats it. Scientists say sharks have special cells in their skins. By bumping into a fish, a shark can "feel" if that fish would be good to eat.

A basking shark lets its food find *it*! It swims slowly with its mouth open. As water passes through its mouth, tiny fish and plankton get caught in its *gill raker,* a kind of strainer.

The tail of a thresher shark is half as long as its body. It uses its long tail to toss small fish into its mouth.

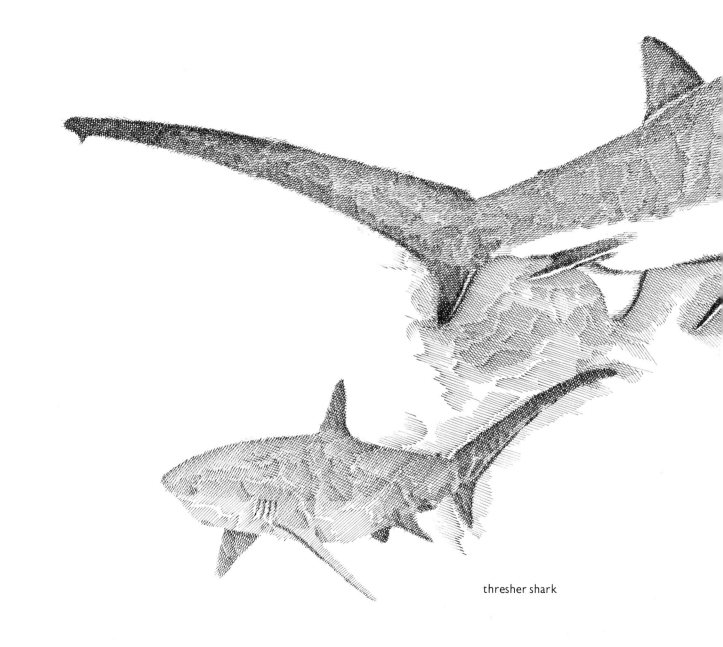

thresher shark

How do sharks use their teeth?

Sharks use their teeth to bite and tear and crush food but they do not use their teeth for chewing.

Most sharks have more than four rows of teeth. The teeth in the front row do all the work. New teeth move up from the row behind. The new teeth push out the teeth in the front row.

Sharks get a new set of teeth every two weeks! In ten years, a tiger shark may use up as many as 24,000 teeth!

A great white shark may attack from below. Its powerful jaws snap shut on its prey. The shark's body shakes violently from side to side. Its sharp teeth tear off as much as 15 pounds of flesh.

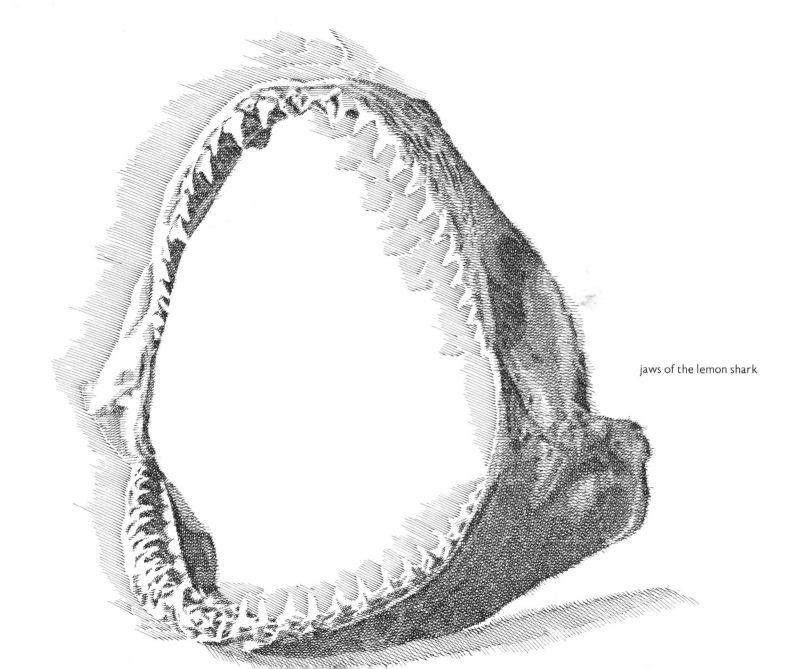

jaws of the lemon shark

What do sharks' teeth look like?

Every kind of shark has different teeth. A scientist can look at a single tooth and know what kind of shark it came from.

Some sharks have teeth that are good for cutting or grasping or crushing.

This is what the tooth of a great white shark looks like.

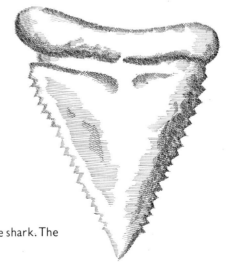

This drawing shows the tooth of a full-grown great white shark. The drawing is the same size as a real shark's tooth.

Do sharks have enemies?

Some sharks kill other sharks. But it is people who are the sharks' greatest enemies.

People use different parts of sharks for different things.

Shark skin is stronger than cowhide. Shark skins are treated like leather and used to make shoes and belts and pocketbooks.

Shark teeth are used to make jewelry.

Shark fins are used to make soup.

Shark meat is eaten by people all over the world.

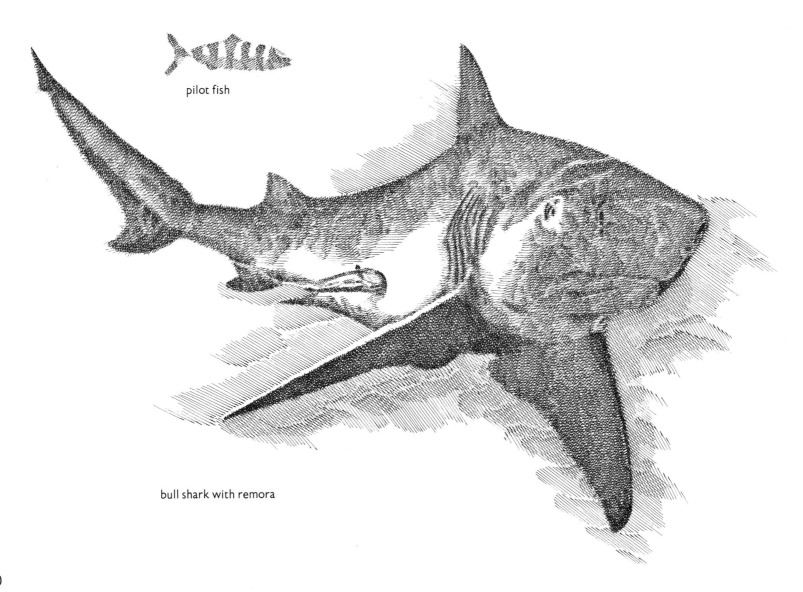

pilot fish

bull shark with remora

The remora uses this disk to attach itself to a shark.

Do sharks have friends?

Maybe you wouldn't call them friends, but two kinds of fish travel with sharks all the time.

The *pilot fish* travels with the shark.

When the shark eats, the pilot fish get the scraps. And the pilot fish is protected from big fish who don't dare get too close to the shark.

What does the shark get in return? Nothing. People once thought that pilot fish led sharks to the fish they feed on. They don't. Sharks have no trouble finding their own food.

Remoras travel with sharks, too. A remora has a disk on the top of its head. It uses this disk to fasten itself to sharks.

When the shark eats, remoras swim off to pick up the food scraps. Then they come back to the shark and attach themselves to its body again. Many sharks carry two or more remoras.

The remora gets a free ride and it gets food, too. What does the shark get in return? It gets a cleaning. The remora picks off tiny parasites from the shark.

When two very different kinds of animals live together in this way, scientists call it *symbiosis* (say sim-by-oh-sis). Symbiosis simply means "living together."

Are sharks in danger of disappearing?

Sharks have been around for 350 million years and it's likely that they will be around for millions more.

Why shouldn't they be? They have hardly any enemies in the sea to kill them off.

Baby sharks can take care of themselves. So most of them grow to be adult sharks.

Unless something horrible happens—like all the waters freezing or becoming poisoned—the chances are good that the shark is here to stay.

What do scientists want to find out about sharks?

There is still a lot scientists don't know about sharks.

Scientists want to find out more about how sharks behave. Then they might find the answers to why sharks attack and what can be done to stop attacks.

They are not sure how long sharks live. And they want to find out why sharks are seen in one place—while just a few miles away, there are no sharks.

Scientists have made tests with sharks. They know that sharks can tell the difference between certain shapes and sizes, for example. They want to know what else sharks are able to do, and what kinds of things sharks can learn.

What scientists learn from sharks can be of help to people. Many scientists are working with sharks, trying to find new ways to cure diseases.

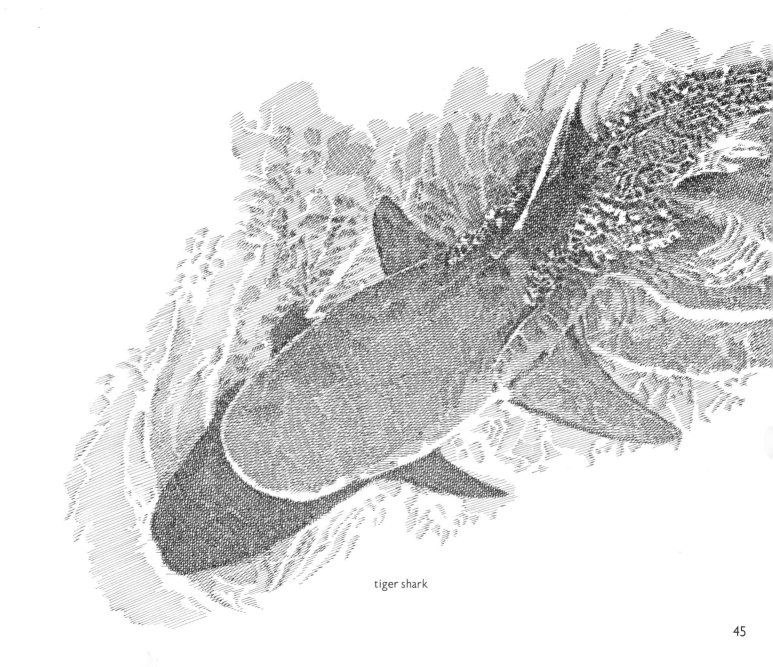

tiger shark

INDEX